CONSULT YOUR CUSTOMERS

Better Management Skills

This highly popular range of inexpensive paperbacks covers all areas of basic management. Practical, easy to read and instantly accessible, these guides will help managers to improve their business or communication skills. Those marked * are available on audio cassette.

The books in this series can be tailored to specific company requirements. For further details, please contact the publisher, Kogan Page, telephone 0171 278 0433, fax 0171 837 6348.

Be a Successful Supervisor
Building High Performance Teams
Business Creativity
Business Etiquette
Coaching Your Employees
Conducting Effective Interviews
Counselling Your Staff
Creating a Learning Organisation
Creative Decision-making
Creative Thinking in Business
Delegating for Results
Develop Your Assertiveness
Effective Employee Participation
Effective Meeting Skills
Effective Networking for Professional
  Success
Effective Performance Appraisals*
Effective Presentation Skills
Empowering People
Empowerment
Facilitation Skills for Team Development
First Time Supervisor
Get Organised!
Goals and Goal Setting
How to Communicate Effectively*
How to Develop a Positive Attitude*
How to Develop Assertiveness
How to Motivate People*
How to Plan Your Competitive Strategy
How to Understand Financial Statements
How to Write a Marketing Plan
How to Write a Staff Manual
Improving Employee Performance

Improving Performance Through
  Benchmarking
Improving Relations at Work
Keeping Customers for Life
Leadership Skills for Women
Learning to Lead
Making TQM Work
Managing Cultural Diversity at Work
Managing Disagreement Constructively
Managing Organisational Change
Managing Part-time Employees
Managing Quality Customer Service
Managing Your Boss
Marketing for Success
Memory Skills in Business
Mentoring
Office Management
Personnel Testing
Process Improvement
Project Management
Quality Customer Service
Rate Your Skills as a Manager
Sales Training Basics
Self-managing Teams
Selling Professionally
Successful Negotiation
Successful Presentation Skills
Successful Telephone Techniques
Systematic Problem-solving and
  Decision-making
Team Building
Training Methods that Work
The Woman Manager

CONSULT YOUR CUSTOMERS

How to Achieve Continuous Sales Success

Karen Mantyla

KOGAN
PAGE

Copyright © Crisp Publications Inc 1995

First published in the United States of America in 1995, entitled *Consultative Sales Power*, by Crisp Publications Inc, 1200 Hamilton Court, Menlo Park, California 94025, USA.

This edition first published in Great Britain in 1997 by Kogan Page Ltd, 120 Pentonville Road, London N1 9JN.

British Library Cataloguing in Publication Data

A CIP record for this book is available from the British Library.

ISBN 0-7494-2147-9

Typeset by BookEns Ltd, Royston, Herts.
Printed in England by Clays Ltd, St Ives plc.

Contents

Introduction

Everyone sells. Whether it's to your boss, your organisation, colleagues, friends, spouse or children – you are trying to 'sell' them something. An idea? Why you should be promoted? Reasons for hiring you? Your opinion, or perhaps the error of someone else's?

You may not think of it as 'selling'. You may think of it as convincing someone why they should do something that you feel is right for them. And it can be very frustrating when you try so hard, and they don't do what you want them to do! Or the outcome does not produce the end result that you want!

The concepts and content of this book can be used by anyone but are specifically targeted toward those who make their living by selling. And *consultative* selling knocks out the image of the slick salesperson. You've probably seen your share of those.

Customers demand the best, they can afford to choose from a great competitive menu and they expect great service.

This can mean agony or opportunity for today's sales professionals. The sales will go to those who best understand and respond to the demands, pressures and profound changes faced by today's customers, and can help them to achieve continuous success. Consultative selling is not a secret formula or technique. It's not a fancy gimmick. It *is* an understanding of why people buy, how to uncover their needs and how to help them succeed with your product or service. This book is not about selling, per se, but rather a guide to *thinking about the customer* throughout the entire sales process.

The goal of *Consult Your Customers* is to help you develop beyond the functional responsibilities of a salesperson and to be seen and valued as an ongoing resource for your customer. You'll learn how positive positioning skills will help you to pave the way for achieving sales excellence. These skills include:

- Having tips in advance on how to succeed before you walk in the door
- Creating your own sales growth plan to help you exceed your goals
- Getting appointments with decision makers; having them want to see you
- Doing an in-person needs analysis; having prospects tell you what they want and show you how to sell them your product or service
- Identifying and positioning to each customer's emotional needs
- Giving your presentation directed towards customer comfort
- Handling objections with a proven path towards getting a sale
- Servicing and keeping your customers for life.

When you have this solid foundation of positive skills, each person – the salesperson and the customer – will feel good about the entire sales process. With consultative selling, everyone wins.

CHAPTER 1
What is Consultative Selling?

The power of consultative selling

Power is a source of energy. Your energy, high or low, often depends on how you feel about doing your job, and the results of your efforts. You will see how consultative selling will benefit both you and your customers. The bottom-line will energise both of you. You will:

- See what's most important to customers, and why they remain loyal to consultative sellers
- Learn how to develop a rock-solid mind-set that will help to ensure your success
- See how customers can make your job easier, by wanting to do business with you
- Identify consultative sales skills and learn how to start using them today
- Be encouraged to value the competition, and identify ways to use competitive information that will guide you towards closing more sales.

What is important to you today?
Since the two most important people in the selling process are you and the customer, let's start with how this book can help *you*. Whether you are new to the consultative selling process, a

veteran sales professional or thinking about going into sales, this book is designed with you in mind. By understanding the consultative process, learning how to do it and making a dedicated commitment to succeed, you *will* succeed.

What parts of the consultative selling process are most important to you right now? Use this list to focus on the areas that mean most to you. In the beginning, review this list weekly. After one month, refer to it monthly. Whether you're new or a veteran sales professional your needs and priorities will change, based on your current circumstances.

Today it's important that I: **See pages:**

- Understand how I will benefit as a
  consultative seller   21–3
- Learn how to develop a consultative mind-set   13–14
- Determine what skills can be improved   14–15, 23–7,
                                                            38–40
- Know how to apply these skills to my
  own job   42–4, 48–51
- Find ways to help keep my customers   85–91
- Develop a plan to exceed my goals   46, 47–8, 51
- Chart my progress
- Select and revise one part of the book to
  support my progress as a consultative seller

Definition of consultative selling

The power of consultative selling starts with the *customer's* definition. Thinking about the customer at each step of the sales process will enable you to focus your energies on the person who can buy your product or service. Here's where the mind-set begins.

Power point: *People* buy; organisations don't. *People* sign a contract or place an order; *organisations* don't. Once you start with this thought, you are on your way to becoming a consultative seller.

The following definition is compiled from hundreds of interviews with customers from every size and type of organisation. Whether you sell a product or service, this definition is a good place to start, and it can be used by everyone. The customer's perceptions become the real foundation of your relationship.

From the customer's point of view, a consultative salesperson wants to:

1. Take the time to understand what I want and need
2. Take the time to understand what my company wants and needs
3. Show me how a product or service will help me to succeed
4. Sell me a product or service and begin a trust-orientated relationship
5. Provide ongoing service to help support my continuous success.

From the dictionary*:

Consult: **1.** to deliberate on: discuss **2.** to ask advice of: seek the opinion of: apply to for information or instruction

Consultative: **1.** having the privilege or right of conference **2.** advisory

Sell: **1.** to achieve a sale: find a buyer

Selling: **1.** the act, process or art of offering goods for sale

Based on these definitions, what do you think are the major differences between the customer's perception (definition) and the technical descriptions from the dictionary?

_____

_____

_____

_____

* Webster's *Third New International Dictionary of the English Language*, unabridged, 1968.

Now, here are the author's comments about the two definitions of consultative selling:

- The important difference is that the customer's definition is based on *his or her* wants and needs. It describes an emotional picture of what they expect from a salesperson.
- The technical definition describes the process, primarily from *your* vantage point, and does not contain any reference to the emotional side of selling.
- Discovering the emotional needs of your customer, and presenting to those needs, are two very important steps in the consultative selling process.

Consultative selling definition summary
- Understand what the customer wants and/or needs.
- Understand the goals of the customer and his/her organisation.
- Offer product or service recommendations, based on that knowledge (not on what you want to sell).
- Keep in touch with customers to ensure that they are satisfied.
- Care about their current and continuous success.

What is a mind-set?

Now that you know what customers expect, how can you give yourself the best start? Allow yourself to develop a consultative mind-set. Let's take a look at what a mind-set is, and then what you can do to get yourself going in the right direction.

Each individual develops a way of thinking about things that happen in life. Past experiences form the basis of how you think, act or react to a person, activity or situation. New situations or opportunities, like consultative selling, provide a need to develop a whole new way of thinking.

A mind-set is your foundation for actions, reactions and deliberate approaches to any given situation. The organised conscious and unconscious adaptive activities are set by each individual. A negative mind-set often develops when you've had bad experiences. For example, let's say that your product or service can help the financial officer in any organisation. You've tried several times but can't make a sale. You may say to yourself, 'I'm not going to waste my time calling on them any more. They never buy.'

You've developed the mind-set that they won't buy. And they won't – because you have eliminated them from your list of prospects. If you know that what you sell will help them, but you don't take the time to understand why they don't buy, you both lose. You lose selling opportunities, and those financial officers will buy from someone else, because you have developed a negative mind-set.

On the positive side, you may have had wonderful experiences in selling to plant managers. Your natural inclination, then, is to look forward to calling on them, presenting to them and feeling confident that you have a good chance to get an order. You feel positive about your opportunities. You prepare lists of prospects, you're skilled at getting appointments, and you are enthusiastic during your presentation. You have developed a positive mind-set about selling to plan managers.

Power point: You have the capacity to set your mind on what you want to do. You determine your own mind-set. You set the rules of thinking, perceiving, feeling and acting in a certain manner.

How do you develop a consultative mind-set?
1. Begin by acknowledging that you can learn how to be a consultative seller.
2. Position the fact that you are the person who can best help your customer.
3. Read and memorise the definition of a consultative seller as viewed by the customer.

4. Make a detailed commitment to learn, and practise the skills needed for consultative success.
5. Set a plan to succeed, and be flexible in your efforts to make it happen.
6. Ask yourself each day, 'What can I do to help a customer?'

Exercise: Are you on target?
Use the terms defined in this section to determine where you are right now. An honest rating of yourself in the following chart will help you begin to focus on your role as a consultative seller.

In dealing with customers and prospects, I:

Point value:	5 Always	4 Often	3 Sometimes	2 Rarely	1 Never
Have a consultative mind-set					
Want to take the time to: • Understand what they want • Understand what they need • Understand the needs and goals of their company					
Value their time					
Discuss what is important to them					
Sell them what *they* want					
Care about how *they* succeed with what I've sold them					

Point value:	5 Always	4 Often	3 Sometimes	2 Rarely	1 Never
Earn their trust					
Provide ongoing service to ensure that all is going well					
Care about their continuous success					

TOTAL POINTS: _____

If you scored above 40, you have an excellent foundation in place to achieve success as a consultative seller. If you rated between 30 and 40, you have a good start and can work towards achieving greater success. A total under 30 indicates one of two things: either you don't know how to achieve sales success (this book can help you) or you should not be in a sales position.

Many consultative sellers may use this rating as a confirmation that they are on target. And they want to stay there! If your sales results are not exactly where you would like them to be, improvement in one or two areas can make a major difference between average sales performance and exceeding your goals.

New sales professionals may use this as a starting point to understand the most important aspects of consultative selling.

> **Power point:** Whatever you do, always think about what you are doing *through the eyes of the customer.*

What consultative selling means to customers

This is the mind-set the customer has about *you*. Once you

show your customers that you have their best interests in mind, many wonderful things happen.

- **They are more relaxed.** There's almost a sigh of relief. The 'sleazy' image of a salesperson disappears. They welcome you without having to hold on to their wallets. They feel good about doing business with you. You are interested in their success and they know it. A consultative seller's customer doesn't think, every time you call, 'What is she trying to sell me now?' They know you won't give them a sales pitch because you need one more sale to be number 1 or to win a contest, or because selling them something is in *your* best interests, not theirs,

- **They trust you.** Customers will be more receptive to listening to you if you have helped them with a profitable sales recommendation and/or excellent service. They will be more open-minded, even if they are not quite sure they want what you are offering. Customers of consultative sellers want to hear about what you have, knowing that the 'what's in it for me?' is targeted for *them*.

- **They have confidence in you.** You have demonstrated that you know what they want and can give it to them. Your recommendations are based on *their* needs, and what you sell works well. If it doesn't, you quickly correct it with another product or expanded personal service. They know you won't disappear if things go wrong.

- **They feel good about spending money with you.** Every customer wants to make profitable decisions. If they have a budget for your products or services, and you've helped them get a good return on their investment (volume gain; increased market share; cost savings, etc), they want to keep that ball rolling! You're less likely to hear, 'I don't have it in the budget' or 'I have no money now.' They will often let you know when they are in the budgeting process, to get an estimate of your prices and make a conscious effort to ensure that the money is there. And if budgets are cut, which happens in all organisations, they will defend their need and the return on investment they have received from you. They will fight to keep it in the budget.

What do your customers think of you?

To evaluate your current starting point, write down the names of your three top customers. Identify what you think they value most about you.

My top three customers value me because:

1. (*Name of customer*) _____

_____

_____

2. (*Name of customer*) _____

_____

_____

3. (Name of customer) _____

_____

_____

> **Power point:** The mind-set of the customer is that you are a *professional adviser*. You help them to make profitable decisions, and they want that to happen again.

Now, let's take a look at these three customers and identify how they have received a return on investment (whatever may be important to them: profit, increased market share, cost savings, increased productivity, etc) based on their purchase from you. List as many reasons as you know.

Then, write down what you have done, and *one more idea* you can recommend, in order to build on your existing success.

1. (*Customer name*) receives a return on investment in the following ways:

_____

_____

Here's what I did to help make it happen:_____

_____

_____

If they did this, it would help them even more:_____

_____

_____

2. (*Customer name*) receives a return on investment in the following ways:

_____

_____

Here's what I did to help make it happen:_____

_____

_____

If they did this, it would help them even more:_____

_____

_____

3. (*Customer name*) receives a return on investment in the following ways:

_____

_____

Here's what I did to help make it happen:_____

_____

_____

If they did this, it would help them even more:_____

_____

_____

By reflecting on how your best customers value you and what you did to help them, and s-t-r-e-t-c-h-i-n-g to help them with one more idea, you reinforce your value to them. Call or write to them today about that one new idea.

Now let's take a look at several prospective customers who have seen your presentation. They expressed interest but have not given you an order. How do you think they value you? What new ideas can you take to them that would help them want to buy from you?

Think about it. *They* have thought about it, and they have not bought yet. Were they relaxed? Did they seem to trust you? Did they express confidence in what you were saying — not give a budget objection before you were through with your presentation?

1. (*Prospect name*) told me that _____

_____

To help them see how they can get a return on investment, I can: _____

_____

2. (*Prospect name*) told me that _____

_____

To help them see how they can get a return on investment, I can: _____

_____

3. (*Prospect name*) told me that _____

_____

To help them see how they can get a return on investment, I can: _____

_____

To ensure that your customers and prospects develop a good min-set about you, go back to the definitions of consultative selling and mind-set. Use those definitions to strengthen your next sales presentation. It will mean a lot to your customers.

How to exceed your sales goals

Consultative selling will change the way you think about selling. And, in turn, you will:

- Retain more customers
- Turn more prospects into customers
- Have customers that are receptive to your calls
- Receive more referrals
- Have customers call you
- Help to reduce sales stress
- Make more money.

Let's face it: we're in a very competitive sales environment. The pressure is on to get the numbers. Meeting quotas and closing sales are part of the daily mental gymnastics of most salespeople. You are paid to get results.

Many times these goals stretch the wrong sales muscles. People think too much about selling. What can I sell? To whom can I sell? How much can I sell? How can I get someone to buy from me? How can I get them to buy more?

Many times veterans find themselves focusing on these thoughts, and their sales go down. What is wrong is that they are thinking mainly about themselves, not the customer. Often, what prevents us from exceeding our sales goals is one word in this sentence: *us*.

Consultative selling will help you to put goals in a different perspective.

What's your perspective now?

When you hear the word *goal*, the following thoughts may occur. Tick the ones that you currently have or have had before.

☐ If I make my quota, I will be very happy.
☐ I'm competitive. I'll beat everyone!

☐ Piece of cake. No problem.
☐ Who set these goals?
☐ I'll never make it.
☐ No one asked me for my opinion.
☐ These goals are impossible.
☐ I can exceed my goals.

Can you identify any customer-orientated thoughts from the above list? That's a major missing ingredient for helping to exceed goals. If you have these thoughts, your next step is to ensure that you shift your focus to your customers. In the beginning, this will be hard to do.

> **Power point:** Every time you think about yourself, follow that thought with something that you can do to help a current customer, or a prospect. This is an exercise for the mind. Your mental gymnastics should always include the needs of your customers.

The expertise of the consultative seller is to always link your goals with those of your customer. Your actions will then lead to discovering customer needs and providing solutions. You will find that providing a product or service to help your customers to achieve their goals will always be a step towards achieving yours.

Benefits of customer-driven efforts
When customers feel that they are dealing with a salesperson who cares about their success, many wonderful things happen.

They look forward to speaking to you
Consultative sellers often work by appointment and/or contact their customers on a regular basis. Since phone contact is very important, a frustrating part of the sales process may be when you can't reach your customer. Frequent voice-mail messages (and so many call-back requests that their computer practically recognises your voice!); 'She's in a

meeting'; 'He just stepped out' ... All this can cause a great deal of anxiety for the salesperson. But the classic situations – when the assistant asks your name, puts you on hold and comes back with 'He's unavailable, not in, on holiday, not interested' – usually does not happen to a consultative seller.

They want to see you
Your customers know that you're there to provide service, and will not hide behind the filing cabinets when the receptionist announces your arrival. They are less likely to cancel appointments at the last minute, because their time with you is always productive, in one way or another.

You will receive more referrals
Satisfied customers tell their friends and associates about good service. Getting new customers is not easy, but the good news is that referrals are the best source for making this happen. In addition, your chances of closing a sale with a referral increased dramatically, based on the pre-selling done by your existing customer.

More Referrals = More Receptive Prospects = More Sales

Your are positioned as an adviser to your customer
As an adviser, you will most likely be called when a need or opportunity arises to use your service or product. You will receive more incoming calls requesting information and/or placing orders.

You will have less sales stress
When you are a consultative seller, you've still got numbers to meet and fires to put out – but you handle them differently. You feel more in control, because you make choices that will target customer needs and satisfaction. Stress often comes when you feel out of control, or when you can't control a situation. You *can* control your *choice*, however, on the best way to act or react. When the pressure gets intense, you won't go into sales frenzy. Calling everyone and anyone, and 'telling

more than selling' is stressful for you, annoying to customers and usually does not result in any significant sales volume. When the goal is to attract and retain customers, your choices will be focused towards that end.

Power point: Ask yourself: 'What can I do that will be to my best advantage?' Then you choose your next steps. *Your* best advantage will be to find ways to help your *customers* and to contact more prospects.

So how else can you benefit besides attracting and retaining more customers? Will you make more money? Count on it. If your pay package rewards achievement, you'll soon be looking for ways to invest your 'unexpected' increase in cash flow. Here's an extreme case: a young woman was hired straight from college. No sales experience. Willing to learn and follow the concepts and content of this book. Her initial sales production was $21,000 per year. In 1993, just six years later, she sold $45 million worth of services.

Power point: The end result is to meet the goals established by your organisation. How you get there and exceed them is often the result of helping customers achieve *their* goals.

The difference between basic and consultative sales skills

Two principal skill areas form the solid foundation for your consultative success: basic sales skills and consultative sales skills.

Basic sales skills are the tactical skills that are required to do your job. Most sales positions require you to become knowledgeable in these areas. In addition, each organisation and/or industry will have very specific learning objectives, to ensure that you learn everything that is of importance to your organisation and the markets you serve.

Learning effective ways to implement these basic skills is a prerequisite for consultative selling. In Chapter 2 you will have the opportunity to begin a self-assessment for the basics. At that time, you can begin to discuss your specific growth needs with your manager. Here is a list of basic sales skills:

Job knowledge
- Company background, history, mission, vision
- Product knowledge, service knowledge
- Sales goals
- Markets for distribution/sales
- Knowledge of the competition

Business ability
- Time management
- Territory management
- Record keeping
- Profitable selling
- Goal monitoring

Selling skills
- Prospecting
- Getting appointments
- Probing
- Individual and group presentations
- Handling objections
- Closing
- Call-back presentations
- Getting referrals
- Servicing
- Communication skills (written and verbal)

Consultative sales skills are the skills of an excellent adviser. They include:

A customer-centred attitude

Put your customer in the centre. Leave your ego at home. Actions and reactions should start with the end goal: the best possible outcome for your customer, and profitable results for your organisation.

What do you think about before walking into a sales call?

_____

_____

Ability to listen

Customers should do approximately 80 per cent of the talking. By listening to what they want and what they need, you'll be in a better position to help them succeed. And ask intelligent follow-up questions. The result? You will know how to tailor your presentation to meet the desired outcome for the customer. Next time you make a sales call, think: 'If I listen more, I may walk out with not only a sale, but a bigger sale than I expected.'

On your current sales calls, who usually does most of the talking? _____

How does this benefit the customer?_____

_____

_____

_____

Flexibility and adaptability

You usually know what you want to do before you meet a customer. Yes, of course, get the sale or get closer to the sale. You've prepared your plan of action. You walk in, and an unexpected problem or situation throws your plan out of kilter – now what? Remember to ask yourself that all-important question: 'What can I do that will be to my best advantage?' Don't think in ink. Everything can change by the nanosecond.

Need to reschedule your appointment because your customer has an emergency? Do it. Don't give your presentation in five minutes. You are worth more than that ... and so is your customer.

When an unexpected situation disrupts my plan, I _____

_____

How does this help you to sell more? _____

_____

Impatiently patient

We are an 'I want it *now*' crowd. We want to make it happen. Many times, your schedule for results does not coincide with the realities of what is happening to your customers. Organisations are constantly changing, like a kaleidoscope. Just when you think you are making the last sales call to close that sale – Zap! The decision maker has been fired. Groan. You have to start all over. Or the budget that should have been approved a month ago has another round of cuts before the final word. Or more competitive bids are coming to the customer. You are asked to wait. Do you have a sense of urgency? That's great – keep the fire lit, but don't burn the customer with your blaze! Let the customer know – both the decision maker and his or her staff – that your role is to help provide the best product or service. And that you will stay in touch. You believe what you are offering will serve them well. You will work within their time frame, whenever possible, to help them do business with you.

Just when you think a sale is about to close, it doesn't. What can you do to help your customer? _____

_____

Solution-orientated thinking

Help your customers by showing them how your product or service will help them to achieve individual as well as organisational goals. A lot of people have ideas, but few people offer solutions. You will position yourself as a valuable adviser if you offer profitable ways to use your product, based on what your customer wants to achieve ... or needs. And don't leave it to their imagination to work out. Let's say you sell a motivational product (posters, plaques, etc). Your customer wants to reward employees for achievement. Instead of just showing your line and how beautiful it is, take your customer on a mental journey. You might say, 'These can also be used in the employee's home. Just think how wonderful it would be, if this were important to the person, to be recognised in front of the family. What great recognition and motivation for continuing to achieve ...'

Select a prospect who has not bought ... yet. Based on what you have learned, what kind of solutions-oriented thinking could you try? _____

_____

The skills outlined above take time to learn and practise. Also, let's not forget that we are not perfect. It's unlikely that you will do everything right, all the time. Don't focus so intently that you forget that.

And it's very important to keep your sense of humour. Humour, though not listed here as a basic or consultative sales skill, can help both you and your customers. (Customers appreciate that; after all, they're human too.)

Power point: When your customer is the centre of your sales universe, your thinking process changes. Consultative skills target the human side of selling. For real people, in real-life situations, your reactions will determine their actions. It's your choice.

How to win in a competitive market

The customer is faced by an overwhelming menu of competing opportunities. There are so many choices offered by so many different suppliers, it's a wonder that customers do any work at all. They are the target for everyone, including you. Offers of 'the best in ...'; faster delivery; less expensive and better quality; great service; and on and on and on.

The global marketplace is only a keystroke away. Being in Brussels does not pose a barrier to buying goods in Australia. Not only do your customers have more choices than ever before, but the window of competition now circles the globe.

Is this competitive market likely to change? Yes. It will *accelerate* − with new products and services yet to be developed, strategic alliances to help organisations gain new strength, and sharpened skills to ensure that downsizing does not mean losing customers. So, what can you do?

1. Be informed

Since consultative sellers serve as advisers to their customers, you must establish, monitor and faithfully update your marketing data. Customers will feel more confident about your product and service recommendations if they know you are well versed in who does what, and to whom − for your industry and theirs.

Who are your competitors? What do they offer? Here are some excellent sources of information on the competition:

- *Your customers.* Consultative sellers always let their customers know that they are constantly researching the market. This is a major credential for offering guidance and advice. Become familiar with the products and services your customers offer, so you can help them to serve *their* customers. Work with each one, letting them know that you are always looking for leading-edge information. Ask them, 'If you receive anything that might be of interest to you, I would appreciate getting a copy for my file.' This helps to keep your fingers on the pulse of the needs of your customers and their market. And when they send you something, fax a 'thank-you' the same day.
- *Trade associations.* These organisations do research on your products or services and those of your customers. How do

you find out about trade associations? Your organisation may have all this information in its marketing department. Use your library, too. A main branch usually has good trade information in the business section. Ask the librarian for the *Directory of British Trade Associations*. Join the trade association that supports your products/services; it's well worth the investment. Read their periodicals, use the member benefits, and if possible, go to their annual conference. In addition to the learning opportunities, you can stop and shop at any exhibitor stand to get the latest information on the competition.

- *Business communications.* It will serve you well to subscribe to one or two generic business services, to keep up to date on what's happening in the business world. Many of these services are available through on-line access or in a print subscription. This will help you to keep on top of developments that might have a short- or long-term impact on your business and your customers.

- *Local chamber of commerce or branch of trade association.* You can attend special meetings based on topics of interest to you. If you travel, there may be reciprocal agreements allowing you to attend out-of-town meetings, at member prices. You can network with others to hear what they're doing, what's working and why, what's not working and why not, what the future looks like and so on. Also, it distinguishes you as someone who is interested in learning about the playing field.

By being informed, you'll gain a competitive advantage by knowing what you're up against; how your product or service compares with the competition; and what specific advantages might appeal to your customers. Consultative sellers devote at least one hour per week to keeping up to date.

After you gather information, prepare the following summary. Be sure to keep it up to date as new products and/or services enter your marketplace.

My competitors **What they offer** **Advantages to customers**

———————————————————————————

———————————————————————————

———————————————————————————

(Prepare additional pages as needed.)

To ensure that you know every benefit you can offer your customers, include your own products, services and special handling of customer needs in the summary.

My product/service **What I offer** **Advantages to customers**

———————————————————————————

———————————————————————————

———————————————————————————

(Prepare additional pages as needed.)

Competition creates excellence. Athletes know the top scores and achievements of the winners. They identify what they can do, and then set out to be better. Their formula for winning is based on knowing what skill proficiency is needed, knowing the playing field (who's on it and what they can do), and practice, practice, practice.

Knowledge + Skill = Your Winning Formula

2. Know the facts
Customers buy your product or service because they:

- *need* it to run their business;
- *want* it to help them achieve personal success; or
- a combination of *both*.

Selling in a competitive environment dictates that you must know customer wants and needs. Be aware of what the competition offers, and be prepared to show how your product will help your customers succeed in *their* competitive arena! You face competition, and so do they! If you do not help them to see how their investment with you will fill the needs and wants listed above, then your competitors will. Count on it.

Don't lose selling opportunities because you are too busy to keep informed and sharpen your skills, or because you don't think it's worth the effort. Don't rest too long. You'll be left in the dust as your competitors speed past you.

By remembering your role as an adviser, you will win in a competitive environment. You are informed and therefore can make intelligent recommendations to your customer. You are a professional and continually sharpen your skills. You can provide what no one else can offer: a totally professional you, coupled with service that anticipates customer needs.

Power point: Either you or your competitors will get the sale. Either you or your competitors will retain the loyalty of the customer. The one who offers the most profitable relationship, as defined by the customer, wins.

CHAPTER 2
Turning Sales Potential into Performance

Your foundation for sales success

We began with the customer and the bottom-line benefits of consultative selling. Now it's time to put the focus on you.

The following is a step-by-step method to help you uncover ways to prepare a sales plan, one that will help you to achieve and exceed your goals. You will:

- Find the common threads of excellence that connect all top producers
- Discover how to connect them to you
- Learn how to capitalise on your strengths
- Use them to help your customers
- Take steps to provide a solid foundation for sales growth.

Because everyone is different, we shall now look at ways to prepare a sales plan tailored just for you. You will be able to identify what you need to prepare your plan, and tips to make it work.

Finally, you will see how to set up a plan that will benefit both you and your customers.

Four keys for guaranteed success
You may be thinking to yourself, 'Guaranteed? How can

anything in sales be guaranteed?' It is, when you take a look at the profile of a consistently successful salesperson. Here are the four keys held by every top producer:

1. Positive attitude
2. Extraordinary work ethic
3. Excellent selling skills
4. 360° product/service knowledge

What is so wonderful and real about these keys is that *you* can control your level of achievement for each one! Let's put each key under a spotlight to see where you are right now, where you need to go and how to get there.

1. Positive thinking
Your attitude can make or break you. As a salesperson, you are more emotionally charged than just about any other professional specialist. When things are going well, you feel great! You don't have to try hard to get yourself 'up'. You're already there!

Your work puts you in many different situations and causes pressures that are often beyond your control. How can you stay 'up' when there are so many things that can bring you 'down'? Let's start by examining how you react in the following situations:

Situation	Here's how I react
Cancelled appointments	
Can't get in to see enough prospects	
Increased competition	
Pressure from my manager	
Hearing a lot of noes	
Company makes a mistake with my order	
Frequent reorganisation in my company	

Situation	**Here's how I react**
Frequent reorganisation within my customers' and prospects' company_____	
My product or service is not as good as my competitors'_____	
Add your own:_____	

_____

These are real-world, everyday pressures faced by most salespeople. What can you do to help yourself? First, recognise that a negative attitude is often the result of frustration. Having a positive attitude is not easy, especially when appointments are cancelled or a 'firm' sale turns into no sale. But that's when a positive mind-set becomes invaluable. You can develop a way of thinking that puts you in control. You can make a list of things you can and can't control. How you choose your next action or reaction to the 'can't control' situation will often make a major difference in your sales performance.

Your next move is your choice – positive or negative – and your reaction will determine your action. *You* are in control of the next step.

How would you like to be the next customer contacted by a salesperson with a negative attitude? Think about this for a minute or two. Give yourself a little breathing time to regroup and plan your next step. It's okay to feel down; everyone does at one time or another. It's how you pick yourself up that can make all the difference in the world. The key question to ask yourself, and one that will sound familiar, is:

What can I do that will be to my best advantage?

Successful salespeople are constantly challenged by having to answer this question. It takes a lot of self-discipline and internal motivation to pump yourself up and avoid self-pity. Ask yourself the key question, and think of just *one* way to help yourself with *one* customer or prospect.

For example, let's say you've worked for six months to close a particular sale. It's just about to close ... you thought. Then you get a phone call informing you that your decision maker has just been fired. Someone else has taken his place. You're told to call back in a month. Here is your action: When a new person is hired, you won't know his or her wants or needs. If you know that your product or service has real benefits for the organisation, it's time for you to take action. Send an introductory letter to the new decision maker; include a concept summary of your products or services, a brief highlight of potential benefits and a respectful request for an appointment. Be sure to mention that you will follow up with a telephone call to schedule a convenient time.

You know your own real-life situations. List three negative situations that you've recently encountered. What can you do now that will be to your customer's best advantage (and yours)?

Here is what happened   **How I can help the customer**

1. _____

   _____

2. _____

   _____

3. _____

   _____

Now watch your attitude barometer improve as you start to take positive action that will help you to close more sales.

2. Extraordinary work ethic
All successful salespeople realise that this is a major key to success, but what exactly does *extraordinary* mean? The key is:

Do whatever it takes to get the results you want and/or need.

Extraordinary, as related to sales doesn't mean that you have to physically exhaust yourself every day in order to show how busy you are. That's not extraordinary, that's kidding yourself. *Doing whatever it takes* means a number of different things:

- Starting earlier in the day
- Devoting time to planning for each call *before* the call
- Scheduling enough quality calls (existing customers and prospects who can buy)
- Following through on service requests from your customers
- Thinking of new ways to help your company market your products or services
- Continuing to give your best efforts throughout the day, especially when you've had success early in the day
- Remembering and following the classic motto, 'One more call'.

Successful salespeople are not perfect. No one is. If you have a bad day, recognise it as such and deal with it as best you can. Just do your best.

Power point: The major difference between average and excellent sales performers is that the excellent performers are willing and determined to do whatever it takes to get the job done ... and done right.

There is no '9 to 5' clock for an extraordinary work ethic. You don't have to be a workaholic or tell everyone how hard you are working. Your work ethic is translated into what you do with your time; how much of it is devoted to achieving customer, personal and organisation goals; and your ultimate results. They're all linked together. Just when you think you can't make one more call, make it.

3. Excellent selling skills
Earlier, we defined both basic and consultative selling skills. Excellence in both areas will give you an incredible competitive advantage – you'll be the best you can be!

Most times when a salesperson goes into a slump, the problem starts with the basics. Ask a veteran. An honest answer will usually acknowledge this fact. The key here is:

Having excellent basic skills is the prerequisite
for achieving consultative selling success

You can't have one without the other! Once you determine your proficiencies in each area you can list the skills that need improvement. Discuss them with your manager and your colleagues. Get their recommendations on how to achieve excellence.

Excellent selling skills coupled with consultative sales skills equal your 'degree' in sales excellence. These skills can be learned and reinforced with on-the-job experience. And, like any successful professional, you must always stay informed about any new developments that will affect your sales.

Use resources that will enable you to stay informed or learn new skills. Use books, audios, videos, on-line services and distance-learning opportunities. Target at least one resource to keep you up to date and refreshed on all aspects of professional selling.

Continually successful salespeople (the key here is 'continually') never think they know it all. They know that excellent selling skills are critical to their success. Also, they are eager to learn – from customers, associates, or self-directed initiative – and find ways to stay sharp.

4. 360° product/service knowledge

'360°' means that you know and understand everything about your products and services. Your 360° circle of information includes knowing why your products/services were created (to fill a need?); what they can do for customers; what aspects give you a competitive edge; what customer-support services are in place and how they work to serve the needs of your customers. You come full circle when you learn about what you sell and how it helps your customers.

To top salespeople, 'Knowledge is power' is more than just a saying. You want and need to know everything about your products or services; surface knowledge just won't do. Total knowledge gives you the solid foundation to advise your customers on every feature, advantage and benefit of using your company. If *you* don't have all the facts and understand how your products/services will help your customers, how will *they* know?

Some important aspects of product/service knowledge are listed below. Tick off your knowledge and understanding in each area. For any aspect that may be unclear, get the answers from your manager or an appropriate individual in your company. Make this list for each product or service you sell.

Name of product	I know it	I need to know more
1. I understand why the product was created	☐	☐
2. I know the needs it fills for my customer	☐	☐
3. I know how it is developed and its quality	☐	☐
4. I know the features (facts) about it	☐	☐
5. I can list all the advantages to customers	☐	☐
6. I know how it compares with competitive products and services	☐	☐

Equipped with this information, sales professionals become credible, respected advisers to their customers. Because you are well informed, you come across as knowledgeable. You can give recommendations based in facts, not hype. Decisions are made on the facts that you provide. If you need to learn more, just do it.

Evaluate your strengths

Many salespeople get discouraged about their ability to plan for personal growth. Their plans usually begin with a 'weak' area that needs improvement which often places them in a less-than-confident starting position. My philosophy is to initiate growth with a strong foundation: your existing strengths. This starts you off with confidence knowing that you do certain things very well.

Exercise
Chart your strengths
In this exercise you will do a self-assessment and identify your top strengths. For each item in the following chart, put a under the rating that you think reflects your current proficiency. Put a * next to those areas where you are strong now.

Ingredients for success =
Current strengths + Additional knowledge/skills

Ingredients	Good	Poor	Strong now
Positive attitude	□	□	□
Work ethic	□	□	□
Job knowledge	□	□	□
Knowledge of my company	□	□	□
Product and service knowledge	□	□	□
Markets for distribution/sales	□	□	□
Knowledge of competition	□	□	□
Business ability	□	□	□
Time management	□	□	□
Territory management	□	□	□
Profitable selling	□	□	□
Goal monitoring	□	□	□
Basic selling skills			
Prospecting	□	□	□
Presenting to enough prospects	□	□	□
Probing	□	□	□
Individual presentations	□	□	□
Group presentations	□	□	□
Handling objections	□	□	□

Ingredients	Good	Poor	Strong now
Closing the sale	☐	☐	☐
Call-back presentations	☐	☐	☐
Getting referrals	☐	☐	☐
Servicing customers	☐	☐	☐
Communication skills	☐	☐	☐
Written	☐	☐	☐
Verbal	☐	☐	☐
Consultative selling skills			
Customer-centred attitude	☐	☐	☐
Listening	☐	☐	☐
Flexibility	☐	☐	☐
Impatiently patient	☐	☐	☐
Solutions-orientated thinking	☐	☐	☐

Now that you have assembled an assessment of your current strengths, list all the skills you rate excellent and/or those with a star:

_____

_____

_____

_____

You are now going to take this information and translate it into a strategy for immediately capitalising on your existing strengths, and start creating your own plan for growth.

Develop your growth strategy

Before you begin this section, I recommend that you discuss the previous self-assessment with your manager. He or she wants you to succeed as much as you do – after all, your success is the company's success, too! Targeting your growth strategy, goal setting and planning should all be coordinated with the goals and methods established by your organisation.

A strategy consists of preparing a plan towards a goal. Being by identifying your goals. You need to define what they are, write them down and review them on a regular (weekly) basis. And *take action* to help you reach them.

Your initial strategy starts with a realistic plan

Personal professional development plans often fail for two reasons:

1. You adopt a 'one size fits all' model for learning, coupled with recommended, specific time frames for accomplishment. To help *your* plan succeed, *you* will help to design it, based on what *you* want to improve.
2. You try to develop too many ideas at the same time.

People often get discouraged because they don't know where to start. Don't try to implement a lot of ideas and suggestions all at once. To help yourself grow, select one or two development areas that are most important to you right now. In this plan, you will give yourself the opportunity to become proficient in just these chosen one or two. Remember this about your plan:

- You are unique. The beginning of your professional growth plan depends on where you are today. And that's the best place to start.
- Take bite-size pieces in your professional development growth strategy.

Keep these ideas in mind, and your plan (strategy) will be doable because you will target one or two areas at a time. The end result (goal) is to strengthen existing skills, learn new ones and become proficient in using them. That takes target practice and reinforcement.

Your growth strategy starts here

Capitalise on your *strengths*
Improve your *proficiency in basic and consultative selling skills*
Reinforce your *positive attitude*
Enhance your *work ethic*

Capitalise on your strengths
Write down two of your excellent-rated strengths and/or knowledge areas:

_____

_____

and then ask yourself these questions:

1. How have you used these skills to help close a sale?_____

_____

2. Have these skills helped you to secure a new customer? If so, how?_____

_____

3. What about *keeping* a customer? When did these skills/ knowledge work to your advantage?_____

_____

4. Why do you think these skills work so well? _____

_____

5. What can you do to use these skills with the appointments, presentations and/or service calls you make this week? How can they be used for the customers' advantage, and yours?_____

_____

_____

Improve your proficiency in basic and consultative selling skills
It is important that your strategy include several areas that are 'open for growth'.

List the two *basic selling skill areas* (refer to pages 23–4) that you would like to start with (this week):

1. _____

2. _____

Which of these resources can you use to help you improve your proficiency?

   a. Your manager
   b. Other salespeople
   c. Self-study materials (books, audio-tapes, videos, etc)
   d. Seminars
   e. Other _____

Write your selected resources here: _____

By when will you do this? (date) _____

List the one *consultative selling skill* (refer to pages 24–7) that you want to start with:_____

_____

Focus on developing this skill in every sales call. Think about it before you arrive for the call or before you pick up the telephone. Practise doing this all week. Discuss the outcome of your efforts with your manager or peers: what worked and why, and what didn't and why not. Don't get paralysis by analysis. Think of solutions for improvement and reinforcement.

Reinforce your positive attitude
Every day, you have ups and perhaps downs. Answer these questions:

What do you currently do to have a positive attitude?_____

_____

Does it come easily? _____

How do you reinforce it?_____

_____

When it does not work or you are feeling down, how do you pull yourself up? _____

_____

If that does not work, what else can you do? _____

_____

What one thing do you think would help to reinforce a positive attitude? (List something you can control and/or a choice you can make.) _____

_____

Do it. Keep doing it. Do it even when you don't feel like doing it.

Enhance your work ethic
You can enhance your work ethic by increasing or changing your motivation. Self-motivation is the end result of many different ingredients. Let's take a look at some facts about motivation.

- You determine your level of motivation.
- What motivates you (or not) are these realities: your work environment; your personal environment; your desire to succeed (career and/or financial reward and recognition); what you like or don't like to do; your belief in the rewards of your efforts.

1. Add your own motivators: _____

_____

2. What do you like about your work? _____

_____

3. How does this spark a fire within you to do more?_____

_____

4. Could you do more of it?_____If yes, what could you do? _____

5. How would this help you? _____

_____

Probably no one loves every aspect of his or her job. Often we are not motivated because we dislike certain parts of the job – for instance, setting up appointments by telephone; prospecting; cold calls; administrative responsibilities; objection handling; uncertainty; change; handling complaints. The list can go on and on.

What else would you add?_____

_____

Identify your demotivators

It's important to recognise any or all of your demotivators and what makes them work for or against you. By being honest and identifying what you don't like, you take another step towards improving your work ethic! Identifying the problems helps to solve them. And it becomes part of your plan for growth and improvement.

My demotivators:

1. What do you dislike, or what makes you fell less confident?

_____

2. What do you do when you face this situation?_____

_____

3. What can help you to improve in this area? (Something that is within your control or choice of action.)_____

_____

4. What assistance would be helpful? _____

_____

Use your ideas for improvement and assistance every day this week. Try them out now; don't wait. Give your ideas a chance to work. Get support from your manager. Use your resources – both people and learning tools – for help. You can do it if you want to.

Target your sales goals

You've identified and focused on what you can do to achieve professional excellence and growth. Now, let's look at your bottom-line responsibilities. What is expected of you?

Salespeople are assigned targets to achieve, and often have additional, higher personal goals as well. High goals are good, as long as they are realistic. Realism means having a solid action plan on how you're going to achieve your target.

Write down your specific goals as determined by your organisation, and the time frame for achievement. Write these in ink. If you have additional, personal goals, write these down, too, in pencil. Fill in any areas of the following chart that apply to you, and add any that are unique to your specific job:

Sales goals	Target	Extra goal	To be accomplished by (date)
Total sales volume			
Number of new customers			
Keep existing customers			
Specific product or service sales (list)			
Increased market share			
Growth of targeted markets			

Additional specific goals: _____

_____

> **Power points:** Keep your goals in front of you. Have them visible everywhere — at the office, at home, on your bulletin board, in your wallet and in your appointment book. You want to see your goals every day.

That way, you develop the mind-set to achieve them. You know that you can do whatever it takes to make it happen. You plan to make it happen.

> **Power point:** Every time you help a customer to achieve a goal, and make a sale, you're closer to your target.

Now it's time to put all of these building blocks together into one strategic plan. This will allow you to reach your targets, and give you a crystal ball on how to achieve them.

Prepare your consultative sales plan

Having a consultative sales plan means taking whatever actions are necessary to strengthen your abilities to best serve the needs of your customers. In turn, you will achieve your goals. This approach looks at planning from an entirely different angle.

In this section, you become your own adviser. You have identified you strengths, areas for development and personal sales goals. These building blocks are your steps to success. Your climb to the top will be easier once you set up a plan, and take it one step at a time.

> **Power point:** Your customers should always be the driving force for your plan. You can't make sales without them.

Identify important planning elements

What exactly is planning? It is the visualisation of a goal, a chosen course of action to be followed in order to achieve the desired goal.

What's the purpose of planning? It is to identify both opportunities and problems within a time frame, and allow for development and implementation of actions steps.

What's the best way to begin? The best plans are simple, easy to implement are carefully prepared.

Now, let's set up the model so you can design your own plan. Here are the four basic steps in planning:

1. Establish the goals
2. Define the present situation
3. Determine assistance needed and barriers to success
4. Develop a set of action steps and a time frame for achievement

The combination of these four steps results in goal achievement. A motivated salesperson without a plan is like a racing car driver with a blindfold on. With careful planning, you'll turn your motivation into goal achievement. Planning takes the blindfold off, so you can clearly see your destination.

Consultative sales plan

Designed by_____Date:_____

Note: Use a separate sheet for each of the four plan elements. Set up your plan on a weekly or monthly time frame.

1. *Your keys to success*
- *Positive attitude*

How this will help my customers _____

Goal_____

Where I am now_____

Assistance needed_____

Barriers to success _____

Action steps to take _____

_____

I will achieve this by (date): _____

- *Extraordinary work ethic*

How this will help my customers _____

Goal _____

Where I am now _____

Assistance needed _____

Barriers to success _____

Action steps to take _____

_____

I will achieve this by (date): _____

- *Excellent selling skills*

How this will help my customers _____

Goal _____

Where I am now _____

Assistance needed _____

Barriers to success _____

Action steps to take _____

_____

I will achieve this by (date): _____

- *360° product/service knowledge*

How this will help my customers _____

Goal _____

Where I am now_____

Assistance needed_____

Barriers to success_____

Action steps to take_____

_____

I will achieve this by (date):_____

2. *Basic selling skills*

How this will help my customers'_____

Goal_____

Where I am now_____

Assistance needed_____

Barriers to success_____

Action steps to take_____

_____

I will achieve this by (date):_____

3. *Consultative sales skills*

How this will help my customers _____

Goal_____

Where I am now_____

Assistance needed_____

Barriers to success_____

Action steps to take_____

_____

I will achieve this by (date):_____

4. *Personal sales goals*

How this will help my customers _____

Goal _____

Where I am now _____

Assistance needed _____

Barriers to success _____

Action steps to take_____

_____

I will achieve this by (date): _____

Planning for success is an individual responsibility. You are the only person qualified to design your plan. If you want any assistance, there are many ways to get it — people want to help you to succeed, and they are all around you. All you need is the desire to succeed and willingness to do what is necessary to make it happen.

Continuous Business Improvement =
Continuous Personal Improvement

CHAPTER 3

Preparing for Your Sales Call

Preparation: the key to sales success

You have just completed your plan for specific goal achievement. Now it's time to prepare for the other most important person in the sales process: your customer. Each day, you have a new opportunity to succeed. Preparation will help to ensure you success.

This section is devoted to gaining insight and awareness into internal business operations. This is important for both you and your customer. You'll look at various business functions and how your products or services can be used to support different organisational needs. Then you'll explore the emotional buying motives of your customer, to see how and why they influence a buying decision.

Finally, this book helps you to prepare for successful consultative calls. You'll identify the most important objectives, for both you and your customer, in scheduling profitable appointments. You will then learn how to prepare sales tools that will help you to close more sales.

To give yourself the best chance to succeed, it's important to *prepare*. Preparation takes on different proportions based on the needs of your customers and circumstances. Is this a first call? A call-back? Presentation to a group or an individual?

Each situation requires its own special plan, which in turn determines your timetable for research and preparing for any special needs of your customers.

Understand organisational needs

Even though 'people buy, organisations don't', it's important to be familiar with the basic needs of the organisation. When you are both, you and your customers reap these benefits.

- You are knowledgeable about business in general
- You have a basic foundation to think about how your product might benefit their organisation
- You have a base of understanding and will know the right questions to ask during your sales call
- You feel more confident when you set up your appointments and make your presentations

Here are the basic needs of any organisation.

1. *Make a profit.* If what you sell can help to make money, save money, increase productivity and/or increase market share, this will be vital to your decision maker.
2. *Successfully manage and integrate key functional areas of the operation.* Success requires knowledge and skill.

Major business organisation units

There are many functions and specialists within each organisation. Our focus here will be on the main functions and departments usually found in every business operation.

- **Marketing** This function identifies the channels of distribution for the products or services of the organisation. Who will buy? Who can buy? Who should buy? Who can help distribute? What methods can be used? Which are most profitable? Where should the geographic boundaries end? Or, start?

- **Sales** This is the implementation of the marketing plan. Without sales, there is no fuel for growth and profit. In small organisations, sales and marketing are often combined, yet each plays a critical part in any profitable organisation. Who will sell? Who can sell? Who should sell? What methods can be used and which are most profitable? Salespeople, inside or out, are under intense pressure to produce sales. They are the front line to the bottom line.

- **Human Resources** The most valuable assets of any organisation are its employees. How they are treated and valued can make or break and organisation. The human resources staff need to know about legal issues; benefits; training requirements/needs; how to foster an environment that values and supports diversity; recruiting, hiring and retaining employees; conflict resolution.

- **Management Information Systems (MIS)** This unit controls and coordinates the access of information by both employees and customers. With the global marketplace open for business 24 hours a day, technology must provide on-going specific access and support for each functional area in the organisation, and ways for each function to integrate its knowledge to support its customers. The MIS staff is responsible for selecting the hardware and software to keep ahead of and anticipate the changing needs of the organisation.

- **Manufacturing** For our purposes, we define manufacturing as the group that produces the products or services of the organisation. They are responsible for all final aspects of production. They coordinate with other departments to gather new product ideas, and to design, structure and identify parts/services needed to produce the finished product. Also they must control the quality and quantity needed to satisfy the needs of both internal and external customers. This area usually relies heavily on the use of technology for quality control and increased productivity. If a product breaks or is defective when delivered to the customer, the people in this function often get the blame.

- **Finance** This department is responsible for monitoring the pulse of the financial health and profitability of the organisation. They get very little recognition, yet they are heroes on the sideline. They must support the entire staff's financial needs by providing information, guidance and direction in areas such as budgeting, reward packages and benefits, costs, revenues and profitability. They usually prepare reports to keep each department informed of its financial picture, as well as special reports needed by customers. It is Finance's responsibility to handle all tax requirements and responsibilities promptly and accurately. It is Finance who must often say No to budget overspend requests, unless they can see the profitability of saying Yes.

- **Customer Service**   The Customer Service department is a vital link with customers. It is your partner in attracting, retaining and serving the needs of your customers. The staff in Customer Service must handle irate calls and keep everyone calm. Support services enhance the value of the product or service you sell, and can help to provide valuable information for securing new business and retaining existing customers.

Your customers have to deal effectively and efficiently within their function and must also coordinate with other departments. This should give you a better understanding of what your customer needs to do and do well. This information will enable you to discuss how, when, where and why your product or service will be of benefit to your customer.

Focus on your decision maker

> **Power point:** People usually buy because of one or more emotional wants and needs. They want their purchase to help satisfy these needs.

You may think that because the customer needs your product or service to run their business, you have a better chance of closing the sale. But with all of the competition knocking on their door, why should they want to buy from you? Or, if you have a product that *you* think they must have, but they don't really need it to stay in business, how do you help them to see why they should buy? In this age of reduced budgets, why should they spend precious money on perceived 'frills'?

As you begin to focus on your decision maker, understanding the emotional side of selling is vital. You are dealing with people who have emotional needs. Understanding what these emotions are, how to be aware of them and how they can influence your bottom-line results is crucial to having a consultative mind-set. Let's look at some of the emotional reasons people want to buy. As you do, think about yourself and what causes *you* to want something.

Most often, people buy because of one or more of the following emotional reasons. Some tips are offered on what these reasons are, how to uncover them and how to manage them as part of the selling process. You will read some visual and verbal clues to watch for in your customers.

Emotional needs of customers

1. Ego
Your clues. You will 'hear' your clues. This person will talk about what a great job he or she has done for the organisation and/or industry. They stress their value to superiors, subordinates and peers. They talk about their past, present and anticipated worth for the future. They have a lot of pride in their self-worth.

Selling points. Let them talk about what they have accomplished. Don't interrupt. Compliment them with sincerity on their achievements or value to their organisation. Never, never brag about your own achievements or how successful you are. This will deflate their ego and they won't want to listen. Always demonstrate how your product or service will *support* their on-going success.

2. Power

Your clues.   People desiring power need to be in total control. This person's desk is usually set higher or apart from visitors' chairs. He or she may tell you what to do and how to do it and become frustrated, angry and impatient if things are not done in a certain way. Usually they have major ego needs and they may shout or raise their voice to show you 'who's in charge'.

Selling points.   Don't be afraid of intimidated. Use your own power to direct your actions. Never invade their space. Do not attempt to go behind their desk. Sit exactly where they request. Position yourself as a professional who 'serves the needs of decision makers'. Use power phrases such as 'This product can be used in the areas that you think need it most' and 'You set the ground rules for action. I'm here to be sure that it happens.' That way, you reinforce their position of power.

Never allow yourself to lose confidence because you feel intimidated or less important. They are only human. The worst that can happen to you is that they will say No.

3. Profit/Greed

Your clues.   The person will ask questions such as 'How will this help me to make money?' (or 'more money' or 'save money'). They will usually ask you this first. Profit/greed is a strong emotional need based on performance for shareholder value, reorganisational pressures, pressures from the top and bottom of the organisational ladder, demands for increased market share – any or all of the above and more.

Selling points.   Immediately demonstrate statistical success by those who use your product. Use phrases such as 'increased sales by 30 per cent'; 'reduced waste by 43 per cent'; 'saved £1 million by ...'. Don't tell these people how happy your customers are or that you are the 'leader in your market'. They don't care about this, and it will turn them off. Show them bottom-line results. Be ready with testimonial letters that highlight financial benefits.

4. Survival

Your clues.   These people often talk about the difficult climate within the organisation. They often say 'money is tight'. They are indecisive. Their body language is tense — usually leaning forward and talking at a fast pace — and they appear anxious and fidgety. They are not risk takers and are nervous about making a wrong decision. They are not in an innovative mind-set.

Selling points.   Offer reinforcement that others in their position have valued, used and been helped by your service. Don't tell them your product is new or 'leading edge' — that will push you over the edge and out of the door. Rather, show them how your product has been successful time and time again. Reassure them that you and your product are proven and reliable.

5. Need to win

Your clues.   This person is competitive and usually aggressive. These high-energy, risk-taking leaders of the pack want success badly. They are usually very impatient.

Selling points.   Make sure that what you are selling has some competitive benefit to offer. If allowed by your management, quickly highlight three or four top organisations that use your product. And be sure to point out new or innovative features that will give the customer 'leading-edge' opportunities. Your presentation should focus on how this person can get to the finishing line faster and, if possible, be a star in their industry.

6. Status

Your clues.   Titles are important to these people. They need to know that their superiors value their contributions, and they will work extra hard to move up the corporate ladder. You'll find a lot of workaholics in this area. They thrive on recognition and accolades from subordinates, too.

You can usually sense this need as soon as you walk into their office. Diplomas, awards and recognition letters will be up on the walls, and/or they will tell you about their accomplishments.

Selling points. Achieving status is not easy in a competitive environment, and they need to be assured that what you sell will, first, help *them*, and *then* help their organisation. Tell them stories about people who used your product and how it helped their career shine. Describe how someone used your service; how 'their boss was impressed with the results' will fall on receptive ears.

7. Self-improvement
Your clues. These people want to do whatever they can to increase their knowledge and effectiveness. You may see self-improvement video courses and books on their shelves. They have a thirst to continually improve and learn.
Selling points. Find the proper time during your sales call to comment on what you see in their office. They are proud of their initiative and want you to notice it. Be sincere. Ask them about a particular book or course that you see, and what appealed to them. Ask what subjects they like to explore. Describe how your product or service can add to their foundation of knowledge, help to increase their productivity or help others to realise their potential.

You can probably put yourself in one or more of the categories listed above. Maybe there are categories that you want to add, based on your knowledge of and sensitivity to your own customers.

Set profitable appointments

As a salesperson, your venture capital is your valuable time, and you want to invest it wisely. To make sales, you need to see enough qualified prospects and customers, and that means making profitable appointments.

Power point: A profitable appointment is one that is scheduled with people who can buy or who can strongly influence the sale, or a service call to an existing customer.

Planning to set profitable appointments involves answering three questions:

1, What is your objective?
2. What methods will you use?
3. What are the benefits to the customer?

1. What is your objective?
Tick any that apply.

☐ To set an appointment with a prospect
☐ To set a call-back appointment
☐ To set an appointment with an existing customer

Add any additional objectives:

_____

_____

Whatever your objective, you need to write it down. This is your reason for calling. Write one current objective here:
My objective is _____

2. What methods will you use?
Tick any of the following that will help you to achieve your objective.

☐ Make a list of all prospects who can buy. Add at least 50 new names per week.
☐ Make a list of all current customers and their top three needs.
☐ Prepare a telephone script to use for each specific objective listed above (keep this in view whenever you schedule appointments). Many top salespeople carry this with them on the road, so don't think scripts are for sissies — they're for professionals. You won't sound 'canned', just prepared. Your goal is to get the appointment, not to make a sale. Make your script brief, to the point and full of specific benefits for the customer. Aim for professionalism, enthusiasm, and a respectful approach.

☐ Prequalify your prospects and customers. Be sure you are meeting the right person to help accomplish your objective. (The 'right' person is a decision maker who can authorise or strongly influence the sale.)

☐ Block off time during each week that is devoted solely to scheduling appointments. Do *not* give up your 'appointment to schedule appointments' except for something truly urgent. If you give up that time, your venture capital starts to disappear.

Add any additional methods you use or want to use:

_____

_____

Now write down the specific methods you will use to achieve the objective identified.

_____

_____

3. What are the benefits to the customer?
Why should a customer schedule an appointment?

There must be tangible, profit-oriented reasons for a customer or prospect to give up time to see you. Based on your identified objective, write down the benefits to the customer.

The benefits of scheduling the appointment with me are:

1. _____

2. _____

With careful planning, your time will yield profit opportunity for both you and your customer. This is why you both should invest your time.

Prepare customer-friendly sales tools

It's important to prepare sales tools that will assist you in your sales calls. You want to make your tools 'customer-friendly' because they will be used by both you and your customer to reach a successful result.

The following tools are designed to help you make a focused presentation for selling what the customer wants and needs. With these tools, you will reflect a professional image as an adviser and concentrate on high priorities.

Power point: People make an average of 11 decisions about you during the first 7 seconds of contact!* In a way, *your appearance is the first tool.*

Many sales positions require informality. That's fine – but neat and clean fits anywhere. Carry a professional-looking briefcase, writing portfolio or folder. Don't forget your business cards, pen, back-up pen and your appointment book!

Now let's examine two important sales tools that show the customer that you prepared just for him or her. Treating the customer well from the first, as someone who is important, goes a long way. People don't like to feel they are the recipient of a 'one-size-fits-all' pitch.

First tool: Customer profile

This will allow you to focus on each customer, and the important things you need to know about them and their organisation. A sample customer profile form is provided here; you can customise it to fit your needs. Prepare a file folder containing the customer profile. Fill in as much of the information as you can, *prior* to your sales call. During the sales call, you will ask for and get additional information. Your goal is to have a completed profile. Once you do this, you'll have a better understanding of how your product or service can help your customer.

---

* Willingham, Ron. *Hey, I'm the Customer.* Prentice Hall, 1992.

Customer Profile

Organisation_____

Address _____

Telephone_____Fax_____E-mail _____

Key contacts:

Name_____Title_____Phone_____

Name_____Title_____Phone_____

Headquarters location_____

Number of locations_____Number of employees_____

Primary products/services:_____

Major customers: _____

Important business issues (by organisation and industry)_____

_____

Mission statement of organisation: _____

_____

Specific needs of customer _____

_____

Goals _____

Activity Profile

Date	Action step(s)	Next step(s)	Date needed

Second tool: Priority sheet

This tool will show your customers that you are knowledge-able about their specific function. A sample form is provided here. You may want to ask your manager what to list on your own form, based on the customers who buy your products or services. The priority sheet will be used in your sales call to help both you and the customer to focus on the most important areas of concern. As a consultative seller, you will frequently use this form to help you sell what your customer wants and needs, so keep a lot of copies on hand.

The author developed the priority sheet over ten years ago. Before its creation, the call-to-sale ratio in her company was 1 out of 16. The salespeople heard a lot of noes and couldn't work out why. It was because the customers (and salespeople) had not prioritised the customers' issues. It's hard to know what top present when 'everything' has top priority, and a confused customer does not buy. After the salespeople started using these sheets, the call-to-sale ratio went to 1 out of 4.

Priority Sheet

The following are the current and anticipated priorities of executives like yourself.

☐ Reducing the costs related to health and safety
☐ Developing a total quality commitment with all employees
☐ Increasing market share for existing and new products
☐ Maintaining position of excellence in customer service
☐ Encouraging team building in all departments
☐ Attracting and retaining excellent employees
☐ Reducing costs of production
☐ Entering foreign markets
☐ Other _____

Name _____ Title _____

Organisation _____ Date _____

CHAPTER 4
Conducting the Sales Call

You're on! You have taken a step-by-step approach to get ready for your customer. You have developed your personal plan and prepared for each individual customer. Now it's time to take your hard work and turn it into sales volume.

We will take a look at each major part of the sales call, from the very beginning, to the time you walk out of your customer's door. We'll examine ways to ensure that the sales call turns out to be of benefit to both you and your customer. Our goal is to use consultative skills at each step, and meet the needs of the customer. Our end result is to make a sale. And we will identify ways to end the call that will help the customer to feel good about buying from you.

How does a consultative seller begin?

Breaking the ice is often the critical starting point for the success of your meeting. Your goal for the beginning of the call is to have the customer:

- Be comfortable with you
- Want to listen to you
- Value what you have to say

You are the director of your own first impressions. The decisions you want the customer to make, right up front, are that:

- You are a professional – in image, knowledge and communication skills.
- You have the customer's best interests in mind.
- You are enthusiastic and believe in the benefits of what you are selling.

Tips to help you begin

- Greet your customer by name – and get it right! Everyone loves to hear their own name, but not when it's mispronounced.
- Show respect for every person you meet. Respect is a universal sign of goodwill.
- Be informed and sensitive to the needs of cultural environments different from yours. If you go outside your own community or country, research the customs and ways of doing business there. This is critical and will be an instant reflection of your respect and your knowledge.
- Tell the customer what you would like to accomplish during your time together. Be sure to tie it in with an advantage for them. (Why should they listen to you? What's in it for them if they do?) This will ensure that you are going in the right direction, and will give you the first Yes. If you are going in the wrong direction, your customer will be able to let you know, so you can change direction quickly.

The following sample script is a universal starting point for consultative sellers. You can take this sample opening and tailor it to fit your needs.

'Mr/Ms Prospect/Customer, I appreciate the opportunity to meet you today. As I indicated on the phone, ABC Company has a product/service that I believe will be of benefit to you and your company. In order to maximise our time together, I would like to explain the mission of my company, and how we serve our customers. Then I would like to understand what is important to you, your priorities for (type of product/service), and how our product might be of benefit to you. Would this be okay?'

If they say No, simply ask them how they would like to proceed.

Write down a beginning in your own words:

_____

_____

_____

_____

_____

_____

_____

A lot of salespeople start with small talk before they begin their presentations. Do you talk about the stuffed fish on the wall? The pictures on the desk? The office decor? Okay — but use common sense. Some small talk sounds phoney, and customers hear it all the time. Combine common sense with an enthusiastic, benefit-oriented beginning, and you're on your way to a sale.

Do a great needs analysis

In order to make a sale, you must know what your customers need. This may sound simple, but it can often be difficult to pinpoint. Sometimes customers know the exact specifications of what they need and will tell you. Other times they know exactly what they want to achieve but are not quite sure how to get there. And then, at other times they are not sure they need anything at all! It can be frustrating for the salesperson *and* the customer.

Enter the consultative seller: you. Your objective is to:

Discovering what your customer wants and needs

Here's what you will need:

- Enough time
- Customer-friendly sales tools
- A method to discover wants and needs
- Your consultative skills (Review Part One)

A needs analysis includes everything listed above.

Enough time
Don't rush this part of your presentation. If your customer has an emergency or needs to cut the meeting short at this point, reschedule right then and there. Your words will indicate to the customer the importance of this time. For example, you can say 'Mr Customer, I'm sorry that we have to cut it short. I understand. I'd like to reschedule our time together to be sure that we discuss your specific needs. Then I will be able to give you all the specific information that targets what you want. How is (day) at (time), or would (day) at (time) be better?'

Power point: Do not rush! Many salespeople have a tendency to rush if they are being rushed. If you do this, you most likely won't make the sale.

It might take for ever to get back in touch, and your customer may make a decision based on the little amount of information that you've already provided.

Customer-friendly sales tools
Have your Customer Profile, Priority Sheet and writing tools in your briefcase. Don't take your writing tablet out yet. That will come soon.

A method to discover wants and needs
The best method to discover wants and needs is to use your priority sheet. Remember: Don't come across like a private investigator. Explain what you are doing and why, and the benefits to the customer. If they're not comfortable, they won't talk.

Let your customer know that you are prepared just for him or her. At the beginning of the needs analysis, take out the customer profile so the customer will know that you gathered preliminary information about the organisation. Your goal is to obtain all the information that will help you to focus on specific needs. Share you initial data, and ask the customer to help you expand it, as well as to explain the goals of the organisation.

After you have gathered information about the organisation, take out your priority sheet. Here's a simple opening that you can use:

'Ms Customer, in my visits to many (financial officers, production managers, etc) they have shared their current and anticipated priorities. In order to maximise our time together, I would like to focus on what is most important to you at (name of organisation). Is that all right with you?' (NOW, take out priority sheet.) 'I would appreciate it if you would tick off all areas on this priority sheet that are important to you. And under Other, list anything that is of unique importance to you here at (name of organisation)'

Note. If for some reason you don't use a priority sheet, you must ensure that the customer does most of the talking and tells you what he or she wants and needs. You want to uncover the customer's top priorities. Once you know them, you will be able to deliver a customer-driven presentation.

Sometimes a customer will say, 'They're all important.' You respond, 'I'm sure they are. Which ones take up most of your time?' (focus) Then offer your pen. Be quiet and let them fill it in. This is the first tangible way to identify wants and needs. When the customer is done, review it, and then move to identify top priorities. 'Mr/Ms Customer, of those you ticked off, please circle the top three that are most important to you *right now*.' (urgency)

Next, you can begin to ask at least two open-ended questions:

- 'Of all these areas, why is (state number 1 area) most important *right now*?'

Based on the answer, ask another open-ended question, such as

- 'What would help you to make it happen?'
- 'When do you think this could be accomplished?'
- 'To achieve this goal, what do you feel would make the biggest impact right now?'

Finally, before you end your needs analysis, uncover a long-term (one year or more) question. Here's where you can identify the vision and dreams of your customers.

> '(Name of customer), let's say it's one year from now. You're sitting back in your chair and you say, I did it – I accomplished it. What did you do?'

Be totally quiet and listen. Write down the key wants. You have just completed a needs analysis for short- and long-term want and needs.

Remember: write down all answers on your pad. Keep the priority sheet on the desk between you and your customer; never put it away until you are ready to leave. You will refer to it during your sales call. And keep it in the customer's file for future reference.

When asking questions, listen and don't interrupt. If you interrupt, it tells the prospect that what you have to say is more important. Instead of interrupting, cough! When you ask follow-up questions, don't give off-hand responses such as 'That's great' or 'Uh-huh' and then quickly move one. It's another red flag to your customer that what they have just said is not important.

Benefits of using priority sheets
- Customer begins to participate (positive start)
- Helps to focus priorities (wants and needs)
- Lets your decision maker know that others face same priority areas (comfort)
- Allows you to pinpoint what is most important today (urgency).

The above process has been tried, tested and used by hundreds of consultative sales professionals making over £100,000 per year. This may be a new process or variation on what you are currently doing. Your goal is to make it work for you.

How do you see this working in your current position?_____

_____

How would you adapt it to make it comfortable for you?___

_____

_____

What single skill would improve your needs-analysis abilities? (There may be more, but just start with one.)
I could _____

_____

Do it. Practise it on all your calls for at least two weeks.

Confirm what your customer wants and needs

You've just completed your needs analysis and are feeling confident. You have done a good job asking questions, and you've listened to the answers. You wrote everything down. Now it's time for an important safeguard: making sure that both you and your customer are on the same wavelength. This is where the foundation of your presentation begins. You can't proceed effectively without first confirming that you are heading in the right direction.

Let's start by focusing on what to do next. Do any of these thoughts enter your mind before your presentation?

	Yes	No
I hope I can get done by (time)!	☐	☐
I'll show her the 'hot' new products	☐	☐
I need more sales to meet my quota!	☐	☐
I've got to sell something!	☐	☐

Other: _____

Other: _____

At this point, salespeople are sometimes thinking more about themselves and *really* miss the target. When this happens, it is very important that you work towards getting back to the needs of the customer as you are about to begin the presentation, because this gets you back on the *Yes* path to a sale. If you're on the wrong track at this point, your customer will quickly let you know — but you've got to ask.

Power point: Getting positive confirmation from your customer at every step of the sales process is very important to both of you. You can't effectively proceed without confirming that you are going in the right direction.

You got your first *Yes* when you asked permission to proceed with the needs analysis. To *confirm* the information gathered during your needs analysis, here's a sample enquiry. Like any example, you'll want to customise it with words that are comfortable for you.

'Mr/Ms Customer, before I review the products/services that my company offers, I want to be sure that I understand exactly what is important to you. Based on that understanding, I will provide you with specific information and ideas on how our products can work for you. Would that be all right?'

Your second *Yes* should come now. Customers usually do not object to hearing you repeat their wants and needs. In fact, it helps to solidify their sense of importance. And, if what you say is not on target, they will correct you. That's fine, too, because it gives you another opportunity to ask more open-ended questions. Continue:

'Mr/Ms Customer, you indicated that your top priorities

right now are to (refer to priority sheet or repeat conversational dialogue). You would like to reduce costs in these areas and help staff to increase productivity with the use of new technology. You need to save money and want to provide new training for your employees. Is that correct?

If you get your next *Yes* now, that's a green light to proceed. If your customer says *No*, you can clarify your misunderstanding. Never say, 'But you said ...' You've got a red light and you need to change it to green. Respectfully say, 'It would be very helpful if you would clarify what areas are most important right now.' Go back to listening, and then repeat your understanding. You must get confirmation before the next stage of your presentation.

Practise this confirmation process on each sales call. Put a red tick on the top of your priority sheet or writing pad to remind you to confirm.

On your next sales call, be sure to confirm, and then complete these statements:

Write down what you said: _____

_____

How did the customer respond?_____

_____

How did you feel when asking for confirmation?_____

_____

What, if anything, would you do differently next time?_____

_____

Do it. Keep doing it. It will make the next step of the sales process so much easier.

Give a win–win presentation

A win–win presentation means that you help your customer and you close a sale — and that you are both comfortable with the process. This section will give you a solid foundation for making this happen.

Your sales presentation usually has three objectives. To:

- Create the awareness of a problem and/or need
- Demonstrate and confirm that you can help the customer
- Make the sale.

Let's take a look at each objective and what you can do to accomplish your win–win sales call.

Create the awareness of a problem and/or need

Here's where you repeat the information received during your needs analysis. Point to the priority sheet or refer to your notes, and say something like this:

> 'Ms Customer, you just indicated that (repeat the priorities) are very important in meeting your objectives. I would like to focus on showing you how our (name of your product/ service) will help make that happen.'

Demonstrate and confirm that you can help the customer

Your customer needs to hear that you can provide a solution to deal effectively with the problems, needs and opportunities that have been communicated to you. It's time to *merchandise* your products and/or services. Merchandising is using a specific idea or information to *illustrate a concept*. Good merchandising creates an environment where the customer wants your product, as well as showing them why they need it. Here is the path you want to follow to merchandise each product, service or programme that specifically responds to a want or need. You need to *demonstrate and isolate each product* effectively to spotlight its clear value to the customer.

1. *Paint a picture with words* before actually showing your product. (Describe its purpose.)

2. *Explain* how your products or services fill a need. (Use the needs analysis.)
3. *Describe* the product, how it works and the benefits to the customer. This shows the customer the solution provided by the product – the pay-off. (And answer the question 'What's in it for me?')

Power point: You need to isolate and demonstrate each product effectively to show off its clear value to the customer. Don't show everything you've got all at once. The customer may feel overwhelmed or become confused. A confused mind doesn't buy.

Diamonds on velvet^{TM}

Here's an analogy about merchandising that will illustrate why you must merchandise each product or service, one at a time. It's called *Diamonds on velvet*.

Take a dark cloth (I wouldn't expect everyone to have a piece of velvet!), and take a bunch of silver paper clips (who has diamonds lying around?). Dump the clips on the cloth. Pretend these are your products. You are showing them to your customer, and you want them to see everything. It's a bit overwhelming, right? And hard to distinguish one clip from the other. When you dump everything on the customer, they usually want to 'think it over'.

Now, take away all the paper clips but one. Pretend it's one product. You show your customer what it is, what it can do and its advantages. It's easier to illustrate all the features, advantages and benefits of one product – easier for the customer to 'see' the one product. It stands out, benefits and all, but itself. You make it special for the customer. It's easier to create the environment for a Yes, because the one item isn't competing with everything else.

Now, let's look at an example of merchandising a product: a special report: a special report on marketing. The customer expressed a need to strengthen the company's marketing initiatives, and you have several products that address this. You start with the one you feel is best.

Purpose
Because the business environment is rapidly changing, the need to prepare or update a clear-cut marketing plan is a must.

Approach
This special marketing report is designed to do two things:

1. Provide a step-by-step formula for your marketing plan
2. Provide up-to-date worldwide statistics in all industrial and commercial markets.

Benefits/solution
This report is laced with specific actions you can take to quickly capitalise on existing and new market opportunities.

Confirmation
How do you see this working for you?

Remember to ask for and get confirmation at every major step in your presentation. Every time you merchandise a product/service, you want to know how your customer feels about what he or she has just seen. This will help both of you to stay on a positive track. If your customer does not see benefits and give you confirmation as you go along, you'll probably get a load of objections at the end of your presentation. If you are off track, you need to know why. Ask! Then you can quickly respond with better-focused, benefit-related merchandising.

Power point: Remember to isolate each product during your presentation, link it to its benefits and get conformation as you go along.

Make the sale

If you have taken one product or service at a time and received confirmation at each step, you should be close to a sale. It's time to close.

> 'Mr/Mrs Customer, you've seen how (product) can (state need) and help achieve your objectives. I can start for you on (date). All I need is your okay to get it going.'

Turn objections into sales

Objections can be one of the most frustrating parts of the sales process. Or you can turn it into a way of identifying *why* your customer is not buying. In this section you will learn an objection-handling process for managing any and all objections. This is not '35 Objections and How to Overcome Them'. What will you do when number 36 comes along? You need a way to handle *any* objection aimed in your direction. Once you've mastered this process, you will close more sales.

Commonly heard objections

Tick any that have blocked your sales:

☐ There's no money left in the budget

☐ It costs too much

☐ I want to think it over

☐ I want to discuss it with ...

☐ We already have a similar programme

☐ Maybe in a few months, or next year

☐ I really don't need it

☐ I'm too busy now to decide

☐ We're different

Add other objections that you have heard:

☐ _____

☐ _____

☐ _____

There are two reasons why customers usually object:

● They are not convinced that they personally will benefit.

- They don't see how their organisation will get a return on their investment.

Let's clarify the definition of *objections* and *stalls*. Objections are usually product-related reasons for not buying. (It's too expensive, big, little, green, old, new, etc.) Stalls are usually not product related ('I can't make a decision until after the summer' or 'Call me back after Christmas' or 'I'm not sure my employees would use it').

When objections and stalls are blocking your sale, you must

- Uncover the *real* reason for not buying (a stall is not a real reason).
- Isolate each objection and stall, and handle them one at a time

If your customer tells you they like it, but they can't buy now, they really want to talk it over with their supervisors — what do you do? Realise that at this point, you don't know the *real* reason why they won't buy. Your goal is to isolate each objection (we'll discuss the method for this shortly). You can say to your customer, 'Mr/Ms Customer, I'd like to address each of these areas, because obviously they are very important to you.'

> **Power point:** You must handle each objection or stall one by one. Don't try to handle them all at once. You'll lose.

You will be overwhelmed, and your customer will become defensive. Remember to use the Diamonds on Velvet™ method, and isolate each objection, as you did each product, one at a time.

Thanks to Bill Byrnes of RIA for developing and sharing the following:

The objection-handling process
Do not skip any of these steps. When you hear any objection or stall, do the following:

1. Keep calm

Sit back. Make sure your body language reflects relaxation; don't lean forward or cross your arms. Keep quiet. Your customer may be expecting a rebuttal or a 'but ...' from you, but it's not going to happen.

2. Let the customer talk

Allow the customer to say anything and everything he/she wants. Do not interrupt. Listen, and listen some more. Do not form any judgements or start thinking about a rebuttal. Wait until the customer has finished.

3. Acknowledge what the customer said

Make a very sincere statement, a simple concession. The customer may be expecting you to challenge what they've just said, but don't do it. Example of a concession: 'Many customers initially felt this way. I can understand what you are saying' or 'If I were in your shoes, I could see why this would be important.' This helps to relax the customer. They see that you're not going to come at them with a verbal bat. If their objection seems misguided, don't reveal that you think so.

4. Ask for clarification

Ask some open-ended questions that start with what, why, where, when, who and how. Get the customer to talk. You want to identify and understand what the barrier is. Keep all your questions simple and your tone sincere. Do not attack — in voice or in body language. They need to feel comfortable with this process. Use this type of positioning statement: 'Mr/Ms Customer, I certainly want to understand what is important to you.' Then ask a question about the specific objection — for example: 'While you are thinking this over, what will you be thinking about?' or 'What will be important to make this work?' or 'Why do you feel that your employees wouldn't use it?' or 'Why would it be best to come back in six months?' Based on their answer, ask at least one more question to ensure that you understand what's keeping you from a sale.

5. Confirm what you just heard
Repeat what your customer has just told you. Use the same kinds of words. Don't add or delete anything, just restate it. You want to show that you listened. This confirmation statement is your pathway to the sale, because you will find out if the prospect didn't see how they would benefit or make money. This will lead you to the final step.

6. Conclude and close
Start asking closing questions. 'If I could show you how you would increase your market share by using this product, would you be inclined to give it a try?' 'Is there anything else that would prevent us from doing business?' If you get a Yes to the first question and a No to the second, begin re-merchandising your product, and once again align it with the information gathered during your needs analysis. Keep it simple and benefit-oriented. You should be closer to your sale.

Close with a service-oriented approach

This issue separates consultative sellers from slick, 'sell 'em and leave 'em' salespeople.

Power point: Consultative sellers always let the customer know, before walking out of the door, what to expect from them.

Earlier, you learned the definition of consultative selling from the customer's point of view. Let's review this valuable concept again. Consultative salespeople:

- Sell their product or service and continue a relationship that began on trust.
- Provide ongoing service to help support continuous success.

Before you walk out of the door, you want to ensure three things:

1. You understand the needs of your customer.
2. Your customer understands the value and benefits of your product.
3. Your customer knows how you will continue to service his or her account.

These things apply whether or not you make a sale. Your professionalism and thoroughness will follow you around. This is your reputation and the mark you leave.

After the sale

You want to confirm verbally the three facts listed above. You will want to develop your own words to do this, but keep it clear and totally focused on the customer. Here's an example:

'Ms Customer, I appreciate the time that we've spent together. You have identified the areas of major importance to you, and I will keep your list of priorities in your account file. As we continue to work together, I will update this list as your needs change. I want to ensure that our ongoing relationship always targets the areas that are most important to you.

'My goal is to be of continuous service to you. Yes, I'm happy that we're going to do business together, but it does not stop here. I want you to always be my customer, so here's how I will follow up. I will call you in 30 days to make sure everything is working well for you. Then, I will call you every (name an interval that makes sense for the product or service you sell; maximum time lapse three months) to keep track of any changing needs or priorities. As needed, I will schedule appointments to review your current situation and recommend new product or service initiatives. How does this sound to you?'

Always close with a service-oriented approach that fits your style. What works for you? Write it down here:

_____

_____

No sale today

Now, let's say that you don't make a sale. Of course, you want to keep your image as a professional. Don't walk out in a huff or show frustration (even though it may be justified!) You still want to hit home on the three facts listed previously, and add additional statements of intent.

Following is an example of closing with a service-oriented approach when the No Sale red light appears. Based on the particular reasons why you didn't get an order (wrong decision maker, not enough interest, special circumstances, no need for product, etc), you want to keep the door open for future opportunities and referrals. You can adapt this sample script to your own style.

Power point: Don't forget, the *final* image you leave with your customer will usually be the impression of you that remains with them.

'Mr/Ms Customer, thank you for your time today. I appreciated the opportunity to learn more about your specific needs and to provide you with information about my organisation. I would like to call you on (day and/or month), to keep informed about your changing needs. I will then be in the best position to recommend products or services that might be of benefit to you and your company. How does that sound to you?'

Power point: If you have a call-back opportunity based on specific circumstances, set the appointment *before* you walk out of the door.

What closing remarks would work for you?
Write them down here:

_____

_____

_____

_____

Remember, when customers truly believe that you have *their* best interests in mind, they will keep *you* in mind. When future needs arise, whom do you think they will call? Someone who quickly packed up and left? Or someone who demonstrated consultative selling? What would you do, if you were the customer?

CHAPTER 5

How to Keep Customers – for Life

You made the sale. Congratulations! Now we will look at how to keep your customer satisfied, and foster a value-added relationship to confirm that your customer made the right decision. Your goal is to have your customer for life.

You will consider what customers think about after they give you an order, what's important to their satisfaction, and meaningful ways to let them know how much you value the relationship. Finally, you examine what you can do to help them succeed. You will develop a simple plan for anticipating and supporting their ever-changing needs.

Customer satisfaction: beyond customer service

You've made the sale and you feel great! Now what? Your goal is to *keep* your customer. After the sale, your customer will decide if the benefits of your product or service fulfil their needs. This is a very important judgement. Should they continue doing business with you? Your product plus your personal service will help them to make that decision.

You need to keep your customer satisfied. Before we examine the checklist of actions you can take to accomplish this, let's look at the difference between *customer service* and *customer satisfaction.* Customer service is delivered by you and your company. It is one or more actions taken to contribute to the customer's well-being. Customer satisfaction is determined by your customers. They will be satisfied if you have fulfilled their wants and needs and helped them to succeed with your product and/or service.

You may think that your customer is satisfied because you've done a great job ... in your own estimation,. Don't forget, however, that it is what is seen (perceived) through the eyes of the customer that determines his/her level of satisfaction.

Effective service checklist

Before you walk out of the customer's office, have you:

- [ ] Conveyed a service-oriented attitude?
- [ ] Assured your customer of how you will stay in contact?
- [ ] Advised when you will call next?
- [ ] Asked the customer if he or she has any special service requests?
- [ ] Let the customer know he or she has made an excellent decision?
- [ ] Confirmed that your goal is to keep him or her as a customer for life?

After you leave the customer's office, the ball is in your court. Your attitude and thorough follow-up will determine the level and quality of service to your customer. Here are some resolutions for keeping the mind-set you need to keep your customer satisfied.

- [ ] I will value the relationship with my customer.
- [ ] I will keep in touch with my customer on a regular basis.
- [ ] I will encourage customer feedback – positive and negative.
- [ ] I will respond quickly to any customer problems.
- [ ] I will handle any special needs.
- [ ] I will keep up-to-date records of customer service initiatives and results.

How can you make a positive impact on customer service? Since excellent service always shines, here are some important questions for you to think about. What sets your service apart from your competitors'?

1. When people buy from me, what follow-up do I provide?

   _____

2. What can I do for or give to my customers that will be totally unexpected and appreciated? _____

   _____

3. What can I say or give to customers that will enhance their opinion of me as a professional salesperson?_____

   _____

What happens if a customer has problems with service?

In the real world, problems may arise that make it more difficult to keep a customer happy: defective products, shipping and billing errors, difficulty in using your product or service, and so forth. Be prepared for the good *and* the bad, and be prepared to help your customer. A lot of salespeople get very angry when things go wrong after the sale, and understandably so. You've worked hard to get the sale ... and then something happens beyond your control. What you do next under these circumstances is up to you.

What are the barriers/difficulties in keeping customers satisfied? Write down your thoughts:

1._____

2._____

3._____

What can be done? Write down your recommendations:

1._____

2._____

3. _____

For these situations, you may need the help of your manager or other individuals in your company. Discuss any problems and recommended solutions with them.

> **Power point:** Customers expect you to fix problems. It's not their problem, it's yours. Don't blame others; provide solutions, instead. That's your responsibility.

If you are willing to do whatever it takes to give great service, chances are that your customers will continue to invest in your future.

Keep communications flowing

Your ongoing communication with your customers will have many benefits for both of you. Through communication, you will know when a customer is

- Happy with your product/service
- Unhappy with your product/service
- Receptive to hearing about new product/service information
- Using the product/service in new ways
- Needing help with your product/service.

The only way for you to stay on top of all of this is to set up a service schedule. The service needs for each customer depend entirely on their purchasing cycle and specific needs, so you will be in the best position to determine the timing for follow-up. Some salespeople need to keep in touch daily; others communicate once a week or month. Whatever works best for you and the customer is what should be done. Just do it.

A very important point about communications: always encourage your customers to contact you at any time, for anything. Even when you cannot answer their questions, you can get help from someone else in your company. Customers are more comfortable when they know you will help with any service requests or needs.

Some salespeople hesitate to call and follow up with customers, because they fear they will hear complaints. *That fear will surely help you to lose your customer.* You want to hear about complaints before they worsen, so you can quickly do whatever you can to correct the situation. Don't be afraid that you might not know how to handle a difficult problem. You're not alone, so be honest about this with yourself and your manager. Excellent self-study resources are available to help you overcome this fear. Don't forget — you are an adviser *and* problem solver, and in order to advise and solve problems, you need to communicate!

There are many ways to keep in touch with your customers. You can vary the methods, just keep it going!

- Telephone
- Mail
- Fax
- E-mail

Some welcome communications that are important to customers

- Send a confirmation-of-appointment card before your in-person sales call. Thank the customer for the courtesy of scheduling the appointment, and mention the date and time. This establishes your professional image before you arrive, and sets your apart from salespeople who just don't take the time.
- Send a thank-you letter, note or card after an in-person sales call. Let the customer know you appreciated their time. If you closed a sale, remind them that you welcome being of any service to them.
- If an administrative assistant helped you in any way, send a thank-you note. That extra gesture will serve you well the next time you call. And it's a nice thing to do.
- If a customer has a problem you're trying to resolve, call to keep them up-to-date on the status. It's very important to do this. Otherwise, they will not know whether you're doing anything about the difficulty and may feel that their complaint is not being addressed.

- If anything special happens to your customer – business anniversary, birthday, promotion, special event, etc – a congratulatory message is always welcome. (Many office supply stores and catalogues carry books of perforated, faxable greeting cards.) A note, card or telephone call will reflect your extra effort. Customers remember extra effort.
- Sending a note or letter with a published article that might interest or benefit them is unexpected and another signal that you are remembering their interests and needs. Always mention that you saw the article, thought of them and wanted to see if it would be helpful.
- Always let your customers know about new products or services that have potential use in their company. Your job is to keep them informed. Call and give them the updated information, and/or schedule an appointment to demonstrate the value of the product or service. Refer to their customer profile, priority sheet or other notes, as necessary, to determine if the new product or service will fit their objectives.

Some customers like everything to be formal; others want informality all the time. Some prefer a mixture of both. Match what you know about your customer – sending a formal letter to someone with a relaxed, breezy style is a real turn-off. And be careful to maintain your image in both informal and formal communications.

Some salespeople say they just don't have time to do this, or they hate paperwork, or it's really not that important.

Power point: If you want to keep your customers, stay in touch with them on a regular schedule. If *you* don't take this time, your competitors *will*.

Don't forget – your customers are receiving sales offers every day. Keeping in touch helps you to keep your customers.

Establish a plan to help your customers

In this section, you will learn how to be proactive in serving the needs of your customers. When you are able to anticipate customer needs and offer recommendations that get results, you have earned your stripes as a consultative seller.

Leo Cherne, former Executive Director of the Research Institute of America, made an astute statement many years ago. He said that any 'business owner/manager who is not confused today is not thinking'. Your customer faces a dizzying array of choices, and constant challenges to run a profitable operation. Everyone seems to be putting out fires, spending a lot of time reacting, and wishing for more time to think of creative ways to grow and increase profit margins.

What can you do? You must be *proactive*.

Power point: Alert your customers to possible new benefits, new ways to use your product or ideas for changes that will help them. Your ability to forecast an opportunity or even a danger sign could mean the difference between profit and loss. Customers appreciate knowing that you are looking for ways to help ... especially when they don't have to ask.

Here's a plan: It's as easy as 1-2-3.

1. *Alert customers to published articles that may have an impact on their business.* This says you are taking the time to keep up to date. Make that telephone call to say, 'I just read that ... and I thought you might like to know about it.'

   Suppose you know that your customer's organisation is going to make a major purchase of a popular service. You come across an article that compares the top four providers of this service, and you call your customer. She has not seen it. You send the article and it gets discussed at the decision-making management meeting, and used in supporting their decision. You have aided their plan for utilisation of the service.

2. *Help your customers to network.* Become a business 'match-maker'. Your customers all have unique ways to tackle a problem or capitalise on an opportunity. One customer's skills in one area may be a resource for another customer. Always call your customers before you give out their names; they will be flattered that your recognise their special abilities. Customers need networks of their peers, and you can be a valuable conduit.
3. *Ask your customer on a regular basis, 'Is there anything I can do for you today?'* They may say no, but they appreciate the fact that you asked.

What can you do for your customers today?